Sent	Received

Name _____

Address _____

_____

_____

_____

Name _____

Address _____

_____

_____

Name _____

Address _____

_____

_____

Name _____

Address _____

_____

_____

Name _____

Address _____

_____

_____

Name _____

Address _____

_____

_____

Year	Sent	Received

Name

Address

_____

_____

_____

Year	Sent	Received

Name

Address

_____

_____

_____

Year	Sent	Received

Name

Address

_____

_____

_____

Year	Sent	Received

Name

Address

_____

_____

_____

Year	Sent	Received

Name

Address

_____

_____

_____

Name

Address

_____

_____

_____

Name

Address

_____

_____

_____

Name

Address

_____

_____

_____

Name

Address

_____

_____

_____

Name

Address

_____

_____

_____

Year	Sent	Received

Name

Address

Year	Sent	Received

Name

Address

Name

Address

Name

Address

Name

Address

Name

Address

Name

Address

Year	Sent	Received

Name

Address

Year	Sent	Received

Name

Address

Name

Address

Name

Address

Name

Address

Name

Address

Year	Sent	Received

Name

Address

Name

Address

Name

Address

Name

Address

Name

Address

Name

Address

Year	Sent	Received

Name

Address

Name

Address

Name

Address

Name

Address

Year	Sent	Received

Name

Address

Year	Sent	Received

Name

Address

Name

Address

Name

Address

Name

Address

Name

Address

Year	Sent	Received

Name

Address

Name

Address

Name

Address

Name

Address

Name

Address

Name

Address

Decorating the tree

Wreaths and garlands

Homemade decorations

Gift-wrapping ideas

traditional Christmas dinner time planner

This time planner is based on a 13–15 lb. (6–7 kg) turkey requiring a cooking time of 4¾–5½ hours so you may need to adjust the timings to suit the weight of your turkey. Allow 20 minutes per pound (45 minutes per kilogram), plus 20 minutes, increasing the oven temperature for the last 30 minutes. Cranberry Relish, Hard Sauce (Brandy Butter), and stuffings can be made in advance.

7:30 am Preheat the oven to 350°F (180°C, Gas 4). Prepare and stuff the turkey, then put it in a large roasting pan. Spread with butter and cover with melted butter-soaked cheesecloth.

8:00 am Put the turkey in the oven. Baste every 30 minutes until cooked. Trim the Brussels sprouts, then peel and cut the potatoes and parsnips. Set aside in bowls of cold water.

11:30 am Prepare the Bacon Rolls and set aside.

12:00 pm Put the Christmas Pudding in a steamer over a pan of simmering water. Top up with boiling water periodically. Cook the sweet potatoes.

12:30 pm Increase the oven to 400°F (200°C, Gas 6). Remove the coverings from the turkey and baste well to brown the skin.

12:45 pm Drain and finish preparing the potatoes and parsnips.

1:00 pm Push a skewer into the deepest part of each thigh to see if the turkey is done. If the meat is cooked, the juices should run clear. Transfer to a warmed serving plate, cover with aluminum foil, and let rest in a warm place. Reduce the oven to 350°F (180°C, Gas 4) then put the potatoes and parsnips in the oven, basting every 20 minutes. Make the gravy with the juices from the turkey pan.

1:30 pm Bring a saucepan of water to a boil, for cooking the Brussels sprouts.

1:45 pm Increase the oven temperature to 400°F (200°C, Gas 6) and put the Bacon Rolls in.

1:50 pm Cook the Brussels sprouts for 5-10 minutes until just tender. Carve the turkey.

2:00 pm Remove the Roast Potatoes, Roast Parsnips, and Bacon Rolls from the oven and drain the Brussels sprouts. Serve the Christmas dinner (don't forget the gravy and Cranberry Relish) and enjoy! When everyone has finished the entrée, turn the Christmas Pudding out onto a warmed serving plate. Cut into wedges and serve with Hard Sauce (Brandy Butter).

Food & Drink

Recipe *Lemon Cheesecake.*

Preparation time   Cooking time

Serves

Ingredients

Method

Drink suggestion

Recipe

Preparation time   Cooking time

Serves

Ingredients

Method

Drink suggestion

Recipe

Preparation time   Cooking time

Serves

Ingredients

Method

Drink suggestion

Recipe

Preparation time   Cooking time

Serves

Ingredients

Method

Drink suggestion

Recipe

Preparation time   Cooking time

Serves

Ingredients

Method

Drink suggestion

Recipe

Preparation time _____ Cooking time _____

Serves

Ingredients

Method

Drink suggestion

Recipe

Preparation time _____ Cooking time _____

Serves

Ingredients

Method

Drink suggestion

Recipe

Preparation time   Cooking time

Serves

Ingredients

Method

Drink suggestion

Recipe

Preparation time   Cooking time

Serves

Ingredients

Method

Drink suggestion

Recipe

Preparation time

Cooking time

Serves

Ingredients

Method

Drink suggestion

Recipe

Preparation time   Cooking time

Serves

Ingredients

Method

Drink suggestion

Recipe

Preparation time _____ Cooking time _____

Serves

Ingredients

Method

Drink suggestion

DRINKS

Drink name

Serves

Ingredients

Method

Drink name

Serves

Ingredients

Method

Drink name

Serves

Ingredients

Method

Drink name

Serves

Ingredients

Method

Drink name

Serves

Ingredients

Method

Drink name

Serves

Ingredients

Method

Year _____

For _____
Ideas _____
Gift purchased _____ Cost _____

For _____
Ideas _____
Gift purchased _____ Cost _____

For _____
Ideas _____
Gift purchased _____ Cost _____

For _____
Ideas _____
Gift purchased _____ Cost _____

For _____
Ideas _____
Gift purchased _____ Cost _____

For _____
Ideas _____
Gift purchased _____ Cost _____

For _____
Ideas _____
Gift purchased _____ Cost _____

For _____
Ideas _____
Gift purchased _____ Cost _____

Year

For

Ideas

Gift purchased   Cost

For

Ideas

Gift purchased   Cost

For

Ideas

Gift purchased   Cost

For

Ideas

Gift purchased   Cost

For

Ideas

Gift purchased   Cost

For

Ideas

Gift purchased   Cost

For

Ideas

Gift purchased   Cost

For

Ideas

Gift purchased   Cost

Year

For

Ideas

Gift purchased   Cost

For

Ideas

Gift purchased   Cost

For

Ideas

Gift purchased   Cost

For

Ideas

Gift purchased   Cost

For

Ideas

Gift purchased   Cost

For

Ideas

Gift purchased   Cost

For

Ideas

Gift purchased   Cost

For

Ideas

Gift purchased   Cost

Year

For

Ideas

Gift purchased   Cost

For

Ideas

Gift purchased   Cost

For

Ideas

Gift purchased   Cost

For

Ideas

Gift purchased   Cost

For

Ideas

Gift purchased   Cost

For

Ideas

Gift purchased   Cost

For

Ideas

Gift purchased   Cost

For

Ideas

Gift purchased   Cost

Year _____

For _____

Ideas _____

Gift purchased _____ Cost _____

For _____

Ideas _____

Gift purchased _____ Cost _____

For _____

Ideas _____

Gift purchased _____ Cost _____

For _____

Ideas _____

Gift purchased _____ Cost _____

For _____

Ideas _____

Gift purchased _____ Cost _____

For _____

Ideas _____

Gift purchased _____ Cost _____

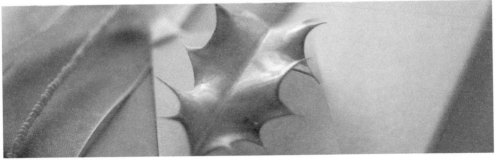

Year

For

Ideas

Gift purchased   Cost

For

Ideas

Gift purchased   Cost

For

Ideas

Gift purchased   Cost

For

Ideas

Gift purchased   Cost

For

Ideas

Gift purchased   Cost

For

Ideas

Gift purchased   Cost

For

Ideas

Gift purchased   Cost

For

Ideas

Gift purchased   Cost

Year _____

For _____

Ideas _____

Gift purchased _____ Cost _____

For _____

Ideas _____

Gift purchased _____ Cost _____

For _____

Ideas _____

Gift purchased _____ Cost _____

For _____

Ideas _____

Gift purchased _____ Cost _____

For _____

Ideas _____

Gift purchased _____ Cost _____

For _____

Ideas _____

Gift purchased _____ Cost _____

For _____

Ideas _____

Gift purchased _____ Cost _____

For _____

Ideas _____

Gift purchased _____ Cost _____

Year _____

For _____

Ideas _____

Gift purchased _____ Cost _____

For _____

Ideas _____

Gift purchased _____ Cost _____

For _____

Ideas _____

Gift purchased _____ Cost _____

For _____

Ideas _____

Gift purchased _____ Cost _____

For _____

Ideas _____

Gift purchased _____ Cost _____

For _____

Ideas _____

Gift purchased _____ Cost _____

Year _____

For _____

Ideas _____

Gift purchased _____ Cost _____

For _____

Ideas _____

Gift purchased _____ Cost _____

For _____

Ideas _____

Gift purchased _____ Cost _____

For _____

Ideas _____

Gift purchased _____ Cost _____

For _____

Ideas _____

Gift purchased _____ Cost _____

For _____

Ideas _____

Gift purchased _____ Cost _____

For _____

Ideas _____

Gift purchased _____ Cost _____

For _____

Ideas _____

Gift purchased _____ Cost _____

Year

For

Ideas

Gift purchased   Cost

For

Ideas

Gift purchased   Cost

For

Ideas

Gift purchased   Cost

For

Ideas

Gift purchased   Cost

For

Ideas

Gift purchased   Cost

For

Ideas

Gift purchased   Cost

For

Ideas

Gift purchased   Cost

For

Ideas

Gift purchased   Cost

Year _____

For _____
Ideas _____
Gift purchased _____ Cost _____

For _____
Ideas _____
Gift purchased _____ Cost _____

For _____
Ideas _____
Gift purchased _____ Cost _____

For _____
Ideas _____
Gift purchased _____ Cost _____

For _____
Ideas _____
Gift purchased _____ Cost _____

For _____
Ideas _____
Gift purchased _____ Cost _____

For _____
Ideas _____
Gift purchased _____ Cost _____

For _____
Ideas _____
Gift purchased _____ Cost _____

Gifts received

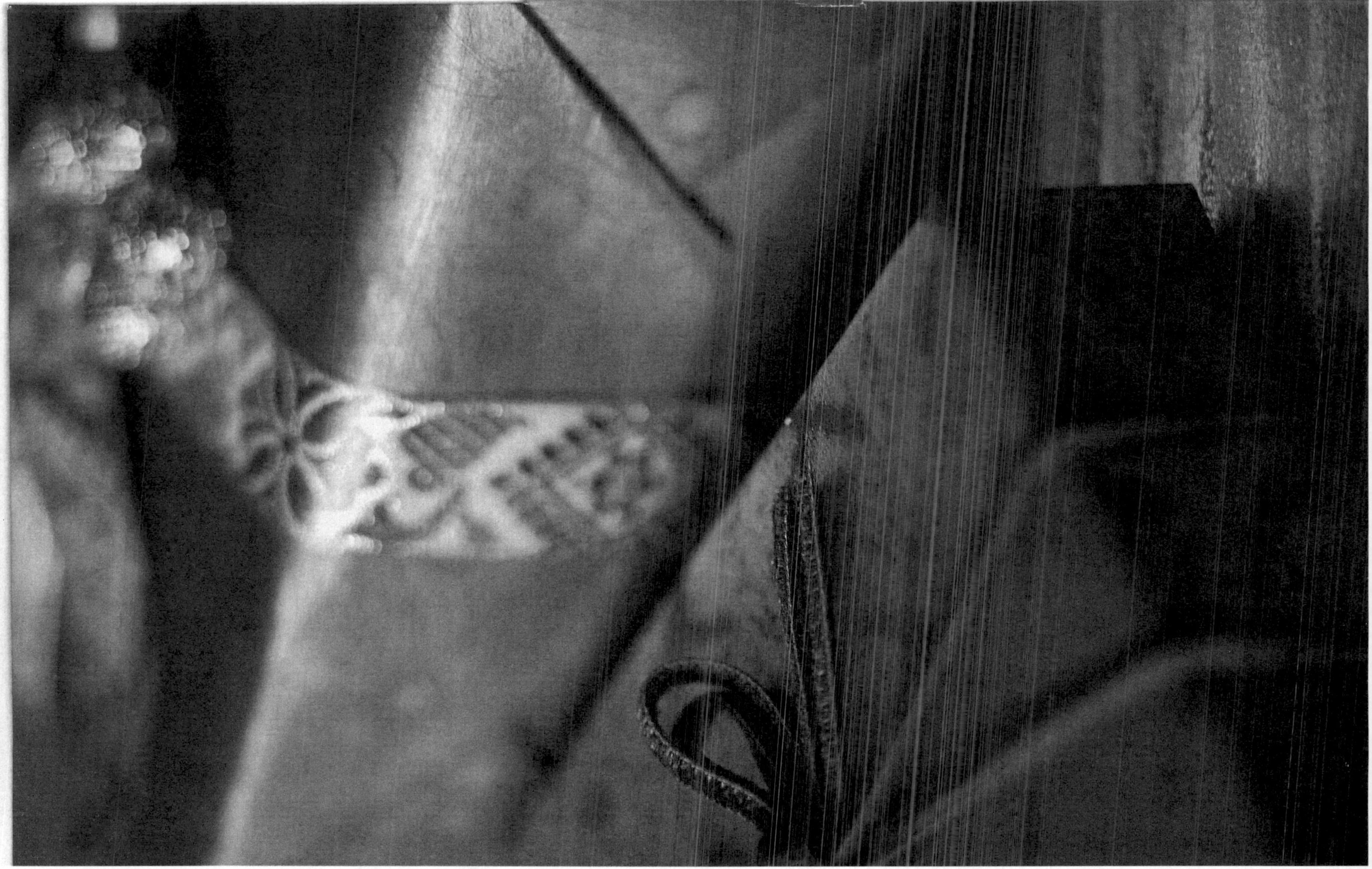

Gifts received
& thank-you cards sent

Year _____ Thank-you sent _____

From _____ _____
Gift _____

From _____ _____
Gift _____

From _____ _____
Gift _____

From _____ _____
Gift _____

From _____ _____
Gift _____

From _____ _____
Gift _____

From _____ _____
Gift _____

From _____ _____
Gift _____

From _____ _____
Gift _____

Year _____ Thank-you sent

From _____ _____
Gift _____

From _____ _____
Gift _____

From _____ _____
Gift _____

From _____ _____
Gift _____

From _____ _____
Gift _____

From _____ _____
Gift _____

From _____ _____
Gift _____

From _____ _____
Gift _____

From _____ _____
Gift _____

From _____ _____
Gift _____

From _____ _____
Gift _____

Year _____ Thank-you sent

From _____ _____

Gift _____

From _____ _____

Gift _____

From _____ _____

Gift _____

From _____ _____

Gift _____

From _____ _____

Gift _____

From _____ _____

Gift _____

From _____ _____

Gift _____

From _____ _____

Gift _____

Year _____

From _____   _____

Gift _____

From _____   _____

Gift _____

From _____   _____

Gift _____

From _____   _____

Gift _____

From _____   _____

Gift _____

From _____   _____

Gift _____

From _____   _____

Gift _____

From _____   _____

Gift _____

From _____   _____

Gift _____

From _____   _____

Gift _____

From _____   _____

Gift _____

Year _____   Thank-you sent

From _____   _____
Gift _____

From _____   _____
Gift _____

From _____   _____
Gift _____

From _____   _____
Gift _____

From _____   _____
Gift _____

From _____   _____
Gift _____

From _____   _____
Gift _____

From _____   _____
Gift _____

From _____   _____
Gift _____

From _____   _____
Gift _____

From _____   _____
Gift _____

Year _____

From _____

Gift _____

From _____

Gift _____

From _____

Gift _____

From _____

Gift _____

From _____

Gift _____

From _____

Gift _____

From _____

Gift _____

From _____

Gift _____

Year _____   Thank-you sent _____

From _____   _____
Gift _____

From _____   _____
Gift _____

From _____   _____
Gift _____

From _____   _____
Gift _____

From _____   _____
Gift _____

From _____   _____
Gift _____

From _____   _____
Gift _____

From _____   _____
Gift _____

From _____   _____
Gift _____

From _____   _____
Gift _____

From _____   _____
Gift _____

Year _____

Thank-you sent _____

From _____ _____

Gift _____

From _____ _____

Gift _____

From _____ _____

Gift _____

From _____ _____

Gift _____

From _____ _____

Gift _____

From _____ _____

Gift _____

From _____ _____

Gift _____

From _____ _____

Gift _____

From _____ _____

Gift _____

From _____ _____

Gift _____

From _____ _____

Gift _____

Year _____ Thank-you sent

From _____ _____
Gift _____

From _____ _____
Gift _____

From _____ _____
Gift _____

From _____ _____
Gift _____

From _____ _____
Gift _____

From _____ _____
Gift _____

From _____ _____
Gift _____

From _____ _____
Gift _____

From _____ _____
Gift _____

From _____ _____
Gift _____

From _____ _____
Gift _____

Year _____   Thank-you sent

From _____   _____

Gift _____

From _____   _____

Gift _____

From _____   _____

Gift _____

From _____   _____

Gift _____

From _____   _____

Gift _____

From _____   _____

Gift _____

From _____   _____

Gift _____

From _____   _____

Gift _____

From _____   _____

Gift _____

From _____   _____

Gift _____

From _____   _____

Gift _____

Year _____ Thank-you sent _____

From _____ _____

Gift _____

From _____ _____

Gift _____

From _____ _____

Gift _____

From _____ _____

Gift _____

From _____ _____

Gift _____

From _____ _____

Gift _____

From _____ _____

Gift _____

From _____ _____

Gift _____

Year _____   Thank-you sent

From _____   _____

Gift _____

From _____   _____

Gift _____

From _____   _____

Gift _____

From _____   _____

Gift _____

From _____   _____

Gift _____

From _____   _____

Gift _____

From _____   _____

Gift _____

From _____   _____

Gift _____

From _____   _____

Gift _____

From _____   _____

Gift _____

From _____   _____

Gift _____

Year _____

From _____ _____

Gift _____

From _____ _____

Gift _____

From _____ _____

Gift _____

From _____ _____

Gift _____

From _____ _____

Gift _____

From _____ _____

Gift _____

From _____ _____

Gift _____

From _____ _____

Gift _____

From _____ _____

Gift _____

From _____ _____

Gift _____

wish list

_____

_____

_____

_____

_____

_____

_____

_____

_____

_____

_____

_____

_____

_____

_____

_____

_____

_____

_____

_____

_____

_____

_____

_____

_____

Christmas day

Ideas for next year

Year _____

Where _____

_____

Who was there _____

_____

_____

Memorable moments _____

_____

_____

_____

_____

_____

_____

_____

_____

_____

_____

_____

_____

_____

_____

_____

_____

_____

_____

Ideas for next year

Year

Where

Who was there

Memorable moments

Ideas for next year

Year _____

Where _____

_____

Who was there _____

_____

_____

_____

Memorable moments _____

_____

_____

_____

_____

_____

_____

_____

_____

_____

_____

_____

_____

_____

_____

_____

_____

_____

_____

_____

Ideas for next year

Year

Where

Who was there

Memorable moments

Ideas for next year

Year

Where

Who was there

Memorable moments

Ideas for next year

Year _____

Where _____

_____

Who was there _____

_____

_____

_____

Memorable moments _____

_____

_____

_____

_____

_____

_____

_____

_____

_____

_____

_____

_____

_____

_____

_____

_____

_____

_____

_____

Ideas for next year

Games played

Family favorites

_____

_____

_____

_____

_____

_____

_____

_____

_____

_____

_____

_____

_____

_____

_____

_____

_____

_____

_____

Year _____ Game _____

Players _____

_____

Winner _____

Notes _____

_____

Year _____ Game _____

Players _____

_____

Winner _____

Notes _____

_____

Year _____ Game _____

Players _____

_____

Winner _____

Notes _____

_____

Year _____ Game _____

Players _____

_____

Winner _____

Notes _____

_____

Year   Game

Players

Winner

Notes

Year   Game

Players

Winner

Notes

Year   Game

Players

Winner

Notes

Year   Game

Players

Winner

Notes

Year _____ Game _____

Players _____

_____

Winner _____

Notes _____

_____

Year _____ Game _____

Players _____

_____

Winner _____

Notes _____

_____

Year _____ Game _____

Players _____

_____

Winner _____

Notes _____

_____

Year _____ Game _____

Players _____

_____

Winner _____

Notes _____

_____

Photographs

Use the following pages to place all your favorite holiday pictures, from decorating the tree and opening gifts to Christmas dinner and treasured family moments.

Picture credits

Key: r=right, l=left, c=centre.

Photographer Jo Tyler, stylist Rose Hammick
Front and back jacket, endpapers, pages 2–6, 7l,
9, 15, 18r, 23–36, 38, 48, 53, 65, 68, 72, 77, 98, 106,
109, 114, 143

Photographer Sandra Lane, stylist Mary Norden
Page 1, 7c, 7r, 8, 18l, 18c, 39, 56, 60l&r, 73, 85l&c,
89, 92– 97

Photographer Carolyn Barber stylist Lucy Berridge
Pages 37, 57, 80, 85r

Photographer Debi Treloar
Pages 55, 101, 102, 105

Photographer Caroline Arber/designed and made
by Jane Cassini and Ann Brownfield
Pages 60c, 90, 110

Photographer Christopher Drake
Page 45

Photographer James Merrell
Page 144

Photographer William Lingwood
Page 113

First published in the UK in 2007 by
Ryland Peters & Small
20–21 Jockey's Fields
London WC1R 4BW

First published in the US in 2007 by
Ryland Peters & Small, Inc.
519 Broadway
5th Floor
New York
NY 10012

Text, design, and photographs
© copyright Ryland Peters & Small 2007

10 9 8 7 6 5 4 3 2 1

ISBN 978–1–84597–495–4

Printed in China

RYLAND
PETERS
& SMALL
LONDON NEW YORK